HISTORY OF SPACE POLICY

The space age began as a race for security and prestige between two superpowers. The opportunities were boundless, and the decades that followed have seen a radical transformation in the way we live our daily lives, in large part due to our use of space...When the space age began, the opportunities to use space were limited to only a few nations, and there were limited consequences for irresponsible or unintentional behavior. Now, we find ourselves in a world where the benefits of space permeate almost every facet of our lives. The growth and evolution of the global economy has ushered in an ever-increasing number of nations and organizations using space.[1]

–National Space Policy, 28 June 2010

The United States (U.S.) has been exploiting space for over half a century. What is the history of space policy and what were the significant factors and events that impacted the shaping of this policy? Looking congruently at policy and events, can conclusions be drawn from this correlation?

Winston Churchill once said, "Study history, study history. In history lies [sic] all the secrets of statescraft."[2] There is very little literature addressing the history of space policy. Strategists use history to garner lessons from the past, and then they apply those lessons to the present to prevent mistakes from occurring in the future. Correlating significant geostrategic events with space policy during the 20th and early 21st centuries will identify trends and lessons learned in how U.S. space policy is formed and developed.

Domestically, a correlation exists between the evolution of space policy and significant events that occurred during each presidential administration. U.S. process for developing space policy lacked foresight. When it came to developing space policy, every administration seemed to start anew. This lack of foresight established a short term view to space problems which resulted in short term fixes leading to long term problems like excessive space debris and congestion.

Internationally, satellite providers expanded beyond governments to include consortiums and corporations which have created challenges. The United Nations (U.N.) is the only body that addresses space issues internationally. Unfortunately the U.N. lacks an interagency and multi-national process to account for the economic consequences or various space policies, and non-state actors involved in this domain.

By analyzing significant geopolitical events that occurred during presidential administrations and space policy development, there are definite trends in how Presidents developed and created space policy. The end of WWII, the Cold War, U-2 shoot downs, Vietnam, economy of the 1970s, the end of the Cold War, Operation Iraqi Freedom, Operation Enduring Freedom, and globalization have all affected space policy. Presidential administrations disregarded historical continuity and lacked foresight in developing space policy for each administration that decided to have a space policy.

Evolution of space policy can be divided into four periods of history. The first was the post WWII and the emergence of the Cold War. Wernher von Braun's V-2 rockets provided the U.S. with the technology to begin probing space immediately after World War II.[3] During the ensuing Cold War, only the U.S. and the Soviet Union were able to access space during the late 1950s and early 1960s. U.S. and Soviet Union Cold War rivalry extended into space, which became another venue of Cold War competition. As a result, both parties initially took significant steps to protect this domain while ensuring freedom of access. The space race, and related space policies were born.

The second historical period was the Vietnam War and the Cold War. As the Cold War wore on, U.S. leadership attended to limited wars, economic issues, and domestic politics, which diverted their attention away from space matters. The Johnson, Nixon, and Carter administrations had a short-sighted approach to space policy.

The third period extended from the end of the Cold War up to the millennia. The U.S. refocused its attention on the space domain. President Reagan was a big proponent for the space program. Star Wars, Strategic Defense Initiative and anti-satellite (ASAT) weapons were part of the U.S.'s strategy under his administration. Space policies during this period had a profound negative effect on future satellite system survivability and the management of the space domain.

The fourth period of history was the first decade of the 21st century - the age of globalization, weapons of mass destruction and the War on Terrorism. During this period, senior leaders realized the negative consequences from past leaders' short-sighted space policy development. The results of past mistakes culminated in a congested environment, actors testing ASAT weapons, and massive debris fields.

United States' space policy from its inception has lacked foresight and each presidential administration's emphasis on space was varied. In addition, the international community lacks an interagency and multi-national process to better manage the space domain.

Space Fundamentals

To understand space policy a basic understanding of the space environment is essential. Understanding the fundamentals of space will assist in comprehending why political leaders advocated the exploitation of the space domain to the degree they did.

Space starts at an altitude approximately 63 miles above the surface of the earth. This is where atmospheric aerodynamic principles end and orbital mechanic principles (Kepler's Law) start. Any object that moves around the earth has an orbit. The orbit is defined by three factors. First is the shape of the orbit, which can be circular or elliptical. Second factor is the altitude of the orbit, which is the distance of the satellite from the surface of the earth. The altitude also determines the rate at which the satellite orbits the earth. This rate or time it takes for a satellite to orbit the earth is called a period. For example, a satellite can be set at an altitude that allows the orbit to circle the earth at the exact same rate the earth rotates on its axis. In this situation, the satellite stays directly over the same location above the equator. This type of orbit is called a geostationary orbit and is optimum for communications satellites (e.g. Direct TV). Third is the angle of the orbit with respect to the equator, which is called inclination. If a satellite is set at a 90 degree inclination its orbit will be directly over the poles. Satellite's orbits are established to maximize satellite capabilities (Figure 1). Orbits of space satellites are predictable, and this predictability makes them vulnerable.

ORBITS	DISTANCE FROM THE SURFACE OF THE EARTH, KM	USE
Low-Earth orbits (circular)	100-1,500	Telecommunications, Imaging, Navigation, Radio intelligence, Meteorology
Medium-Earth orbits (circular, semi-synchronous)	19,000-20,000	Navigation, Imaging, Telecommunications
Geostationary orbit	35,786	Missile warning systems, Radio intelligence, Telecommunications
High-Earth orbits (elliptical)	450,000-930,000	Navigation, Missile warning systems, Radio intelligence, Telecommunications

Figure 1[4]

Post WWII and the Emerging Cold War - 1950s to the 1960s[5]

Space exploration and space policy begins in Germany. During WWII, Adolph Hitler put a lot of stock in rocket technology. One of Hitler's advantages over the Allied forces in space activities was a German rocket scientist named Wernher von Braun. Von Braun was in charge of the V2 rocket program. Hitler believed von Braun's A-4 rocket, later to be named the V-2 or Vengeance Weapon 2,[6] was the ultimate weapon. Hitler's comment upon receiving the program brief from von Braun was "Europe and the rest of the world will be too small to contain such a war with such weapons. Humanity will not be able to endure it."[7] U.S. leaders were aware of the potential of this new rocket technology, and after the war captured von Braun. His knowledge and expertise in the field of rocket science and engineering was instrumental in developing the U.S.'s space and intercontinental ballistic missile (ICBM) programs.

The Soviet Union also possessed the scientists and technology needed to put objects in space. In 1949 the Soviet's also acquired nuclear weapons capability.[8]

There was no turning back the Cold War and the race to dominate the space domain commenced.

The 1950s and 60s were the infancy of space exploration and the Cold War. Both were intertwined and had a conjoined relationship to their maturation and direction. Rockets provided the U.S. with the ability to spy on the Soviet Union and this technology led to the nuclear ballistic missile. The Cold War was the focus of the Eisenhower and Kennedy administration, and it was this war that drove initial U.S. space policy and strategy.

In November 1954, President Eisenhower, determined to make strategic reconnaissance a national policy, approved the high flying U-2 reconnaissance airplane in a very highly classified project known as "AQUATONE."[9] In order for air-breathing reconnaissance aircraft to be effective over the Soviet Union, Eisenhower offered the Soviet Union a proposal to give both the U.S. and the Soviet Union reconnaissance over-flight rights to each other's country. In 1955, President Eisenhower brought Open Skies proposal to Geneva to give both the Soviet Union and the U.S. access to each other's airspace. Khrushchev refused to accept the proposal, but the U.S. continued over-flights of the Soviet Union.[10]

On May 1, 1960, Francis Gary Power was shot down by an SA-2 high altitude surface to air missile.[11] The U-2 shootdown further exacerbated the arms race. President Eisenhower's need for intelligence, surveillance and reconnaissance (ISR) systems to fly over denied access areas became a high priority for the administration.

One of President Eisenhower's classified military space programs was the CORONA Project.[12] The CORONA Project's purpose was to accomplish reconnaissance missions over the Soviet Union. By the fall of 1960, "the CORONA project became the backbone of America's strategic reconnaissance capability."[13] In 1962, during President Kennedy's administration, a second shootdown of the U-2 over Cuba, killing Major Randolf Anderson Jr., reinforced the need for an ISR system to fly over denied access areas.[14]

It was easier for the Soviet Union to gather intelligence on the U.S. nuclear weapons program due to the U.S.'s open society. The U.S. had a desperate need for intelligence about military activities within the Soviet Union but had limited means to acquire it.[15] The Kennedy administration responded to the intelligence challenge by creating the National Reconnaissance Program (NRP) and the National Reconnaissance Office to manage and operate CIA's classified space systems.[16]

In 1958, President Eisenhower proposed to Congress the creation of a civilian space agency called the National Aeronautics and Space Agency (NASA).[17] Congress agreed and space exploration was now a military and civilian venture for the nation. Now that the U.S. had organizations and capabilities to exploit space, it needed to establish policy. In order to protect satellites and continue with the ballistic missile program, on July 29, 1958, President Eisenhower signed into law the National Aeronautics and Space Act of 1958.[18] The law declared that activities in space should be devoted to peaceful purposes for the benefit of all mankind. The law also defined the Department of Defense's (DoD) role in the space domain as being responsible for "development of weapons systems, military operations, or the defense of the United States."[19]

President Kennedy continued President Eisenhower's strong advocacy of space exploration. Notably, President Kennedy also requested congressional funding to accelerate the use of space satellites for world-wide communications and world-wide weather observation.[20] During these administrations, the U.S. made substantial progress in both space technology and space policy.

Internationally, in 1958 President Eisenhower had Senator Lyndon Johnson[21] present to the United Nations Resolution *1348 (XIII)*. This resolution established a committee consisting of 19 nations which included the United States and the Soviet Union to study and make recommendations regarding the creation of a committee to address the Peaceful Uses of Outer Space. The purpose of the committee was to report to the General Assembly of the United Nations on the international state of affairs affecting the space domain.[22] U.N. policies set the foundation for peaceful exploitation of the space domain. The U.S. and the Soviet Union did not have Anti-Satellite (ASAT) capabilities during this period. Space policies were responsive to the current environment and not detrimental to space activities long term.

The events that transpired in the space domain during the early days of the Cold War drove U.S. space policy in two directions. First, the domain of space would be "open to civil space science and applications programs intended to benefit the American people and 'all mankind'" thus the creation of the National Aeronautics Space Administration (NASA). Second, there would be a "need for a classified military space application programs...to improve our military posture."[23]

Vietnam and the Cold War - 1970s and 1980s

President Johnson through President Carter's administrations' policies had an adverse impact on the U.S.'s space program. These administrations' preoccupation with the Vietnam War, the economy, and social programs diverted their attention from space and space policy. The U.N. started to develop policy based on current significant events but did not address the trend of increased number of nations with space capabilities.

The only policy produced during the Johnson administration was the U.N. Outer Space Treaty of 1967. The treaty stated, "Nations shall not place nuclear weapons or other weapons of mass destruction in orbit or on celestial bodies or station them in outer space in any other manner."[24]

As a basis for comparison between the Kennedy and Johnson administrations, the last year of the Kennedy administration, the U.S. launched 13 satellites; during the last year of the Johnson administration, the U.S. launched 10 satellites. NASA's annual budget reached $5 billion in the mid-1960s, but due to NASA's success and the U.S.'s apparent triumph over the Soviet Union in space achievement, the U.S. government and the public turned their attention toward the economy, and Vietnam.[25]

In 1969, President Nixon's administration reduced NASA's budget from $4 billion dollars in 1969 to $2.2 billion by 1974. The only new program approved during this time was the development of the Shuttle Transportation System. During the Nixon administration no new space policies, legislation or U.N. resolutions were created.

In 1963, two nations delivered payloads into outer space—the U.S. and the Soviet Union. This was about to change very quickly and in a dramatic way. In 1965, a company called International Telecommunications Satellite Organization (ITSO), a consortium of 150 countries, launched their first communications satellite. In 1968, the

European Space Research Organization (ESRO) also delivered its first satellite into

orbit. Challenges were arising in the 1960s with respect to satellite numbers,

positioning, control and management. By the end of the Ford administration, in 1975,

11 countries, three consortiums, bilateral efforts between France and Germany, and

NATO had placed satellites in outer space. By the end of the Carter administration in

1980, five additional countries had satellites on orbit. The growth of satellite launches

and man-made objects orbiting the earth occurred at an exponential rate (Figure 2), and

unfortunately there were no international processes in place to manage or assess the

impact these trends and events would have on the future. The top graph (Figure 2)

shows the total number of objects catalogued (documented) as having been in space.

The bottom graph (Figure 2) shows the number of objects in orbit any given year.

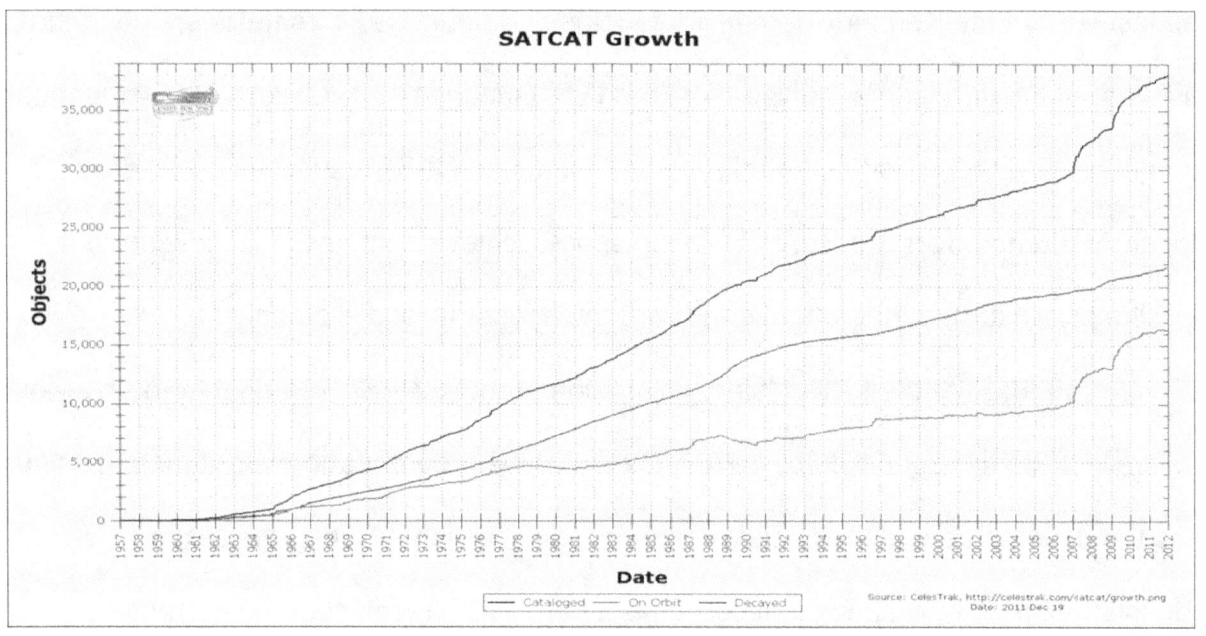

Figure 2[26]

During this seventeen year period there was only one piece of U.S.

legislation/policy set forth by the United States to manage this domain. President Carter signed National Security Council Presidential Directive 37, National Space Policy. Most of this policy reiterated previous U.N. resolutions and treaties that addressed the exploration of space for "peaceful purposes and for the benefit of all mankind…and the rejection of sovereignty."[27] The legislation also included requirements to secure the U.S.'s military space program.[28]

During this same period, the United Nations passed three resolutions. The first resolution, passed in 1968, was the "Agreement on the Rescue of Astronauts, the Return of Astronauts and the Return of Objects Launched into Outer Space" (Resolution 2345, the "Rescue Agreement").[29] Timing was fortuitous since the Launch of Apollo Saturn V mission to the moon was less than a year away. The second resolution, passed in 1972, was the "Convention on International Liability for Damage Caused by Space Objects" (Resolution 2777, the "Liability Convention"). This resolution addressed liability of a space object damaging another space object in orbit. Current events justified the timing for these resolutions. The third resolution, passed in 1976, was the "Convention on Registration of Objects Launched into Outer Space" (the "Registration Convention). As more countries participated in the space domain, the U.N. saw a need to ensure all objects launched into earth orbit or beyond would be registered and the Secretary-General of the United Nations informed of the launch.[30]

In summary, domestic and international processes were inadequate to keep up with current emerging space events. In 1968, the Soviet Union successfully launched its first satellite interceptor, and by 1973 the Soviet Union had completed a fully operational facility.[31] There was no engagement by the U.S. or the international community with the Soviet Union for this dangerous precedent. There was also an increase in the number of commercial entities and consortiums building and launching

satellites. During the Carter administration, 14 countries/consortiums/corporations

owned satellites in space.[32] Neither U.S. leadership nor the international community

had a process to assess the past, present and future impacts of such occurrences.

End of the Cold War – 1980s and 1990s

The Reagan, Bush and Clinton administrations all recognized the utility of the

space domain in achieving national security objectives. Unfortunately, all three

administrations suffered from a short sighted approach to space policy.

The Reagan administration focused on ending the Cold War. President Reagan

increased the DoD budget to pre- and early-Nixon administration levels. 6.2% of the

GDP or 28.1% of the total federal budget went to defense.[33] His Strategic Defense

Initiative (SDI) and other initiatives forced President Gorbachev to "make a choice"

between the arms race and *glasnost* and *perestroika*. No administration following

President Reagan has spent more on defense based on percentage of GDP or

percentage of overall federal budget.

President Reagan also initiated research and development of ASAT weapons

which opened the way for an offensive counter-space strategy. In 1982, President

Reagan's National Security Decision Directive (NSDD) 42 addressed the ability to

"pursue activities in space in support of [the nation's] right of self-defense."[34] NSDD 42

also stated that the United States would consider verifiable and equitable arms control

measures that would ban or otherwise limit testing and deployment of specific weapons

systems if these measures contributed to U.S. national security. However, the U.S.

would oppose arms control concepts or legal regimes that sought general prohibitions

on the military or intelligence use of space.[35] President Reagan's policies directly addressed the Soviet Union's direct ascent and co-orbital ASAT program.[36] President Reagan's Presidential Directive on National Space Policy authorized the development of a U.S. ASAT capability. The directive stated, "DOD will develop and deploy a robust and comprehensive ASAT capability with programs as required and with initial operational capability at the earliest possible date."[37] Further, the directive designated a proponent, "DOD will ensure that the military space program incorporates the support requirements of the Strategic Defense Initiative."[38]

President Reagan's staff was short-sighted and did not consider the long term implications of an ASAT policy. Although, their focus on space was very specific and oriented on winning the Cold War, this approach would have severe adverse impacts on the future of the space domain. Other countries followed the U.S.'s lead in the development of disruptive technologies like nuclear and ASAT weapons.

With the Cold War over, the Bush administration decreased NASA's and the DoD's budget. During this time, globalization and technology had a big impact on space, and much attention was given to the space domain from the international, and commercial communities. Unfortunately President Bush showed little concern for space and space policy until Operation Desert Storm.

In the early 1990s, U.S. forces led a coalition in Operation Desert Shield/Desert Storm. For the first time in war, the space domain played a significant role. Revolutionary technology had produced space-based capabilities used at the operational and tactical levels of war. A few examples included weather data, radar satellite capabilities, signals intelligence (SIGINT), theater missile defense (TMD), military satellite communications, leased commercial satellite communications, commercial imagery, commercial personnel recovery satellite capabilities, position

navigation and timing. U.S. military reliance on space based capabilities in the

execution of combat operations exponentially increased with every conflict following the

Reagan presidency.

President Clinton's administration also showed very little interest in space, and

like his predecessor, decreased NASA's and the DoD's budget. Space policy issued by

President Clinton was very narrowly focused. No agency or process existed to give the

president the breadth of knowledge needed to develop effective enduring space policy.

President Clinton's policy did not account for current and future trends in the space

domain. The National Space Policy of 1996 was a continuation of Reagan's

Presidential Directive on National Space Policy.

> Consistent with treaty obligations, the United States will develop, operate, and maintain space control capabilities to ensure freedom of action in space and, if directed, deny such freedom of action to adversaries.

> The United States will pursue a ballistic missile defense program to provide for: enhanced theater missile defense capability later this decade; a national missile defense deployment readiness program as a hedge against the emergence of a long-range ballistic missile threat to the United States; and an advanced technology program to provide options for improvements to planned and deployed defenses.[39]

The policy was outdated and did not address the evolving space environment.

Until the 1980s the Soviet Union and the U.S. had a monopoly on space based

capabilities.[40] The bi-polar space race gave way to commercial exploitation of the

space domain by other governments, commercial interests, and consortiums.[41] Through

the end of the Clinton administration, each administration's short-sighted approach

created a widening gap between short term needs and long term stewardship. For

example, space policy did not account for the number of manmade objects that were populating space at an increasing rate (Figure 2) starting in the late 1960s. The lack of

continuity and short-sightedness could potentially impact U.S. national interests in

space, and national security.

Globalization, Weapons of Mass Destruction, War on Terrorism - 21st Century

Both President Bush and President Obama faced similar challenges from a

geopolitical perspective. From a space perspective, lack of foresight from past space

events and trends will come to an apex during their administrations.

Both Presidents were preoccupied with Operation Iraqi Freedom and Operation

Enduring Freedom. Both Presidents proposed similar budgets to NASA and the DoD.

From 2006 through 2009 both administrations allocated approximately 17% of the U.S.

budget towards the DoD and 3.5% of the budget towards NASA.

President Bush dealt with the Challenger disaster which affected U.S. space

operations. NASA spent much of its time on the Challenger investigation. The results

of the investigation contributed to the low confidence in NASA during the Bush and

Obama administrations.

These two administrations sustained military space-based funding. The DoD

continued its ISR launches at a rate of 0 to 4 annually. This has been the standard

launch rate for DoD satellites for the past two decades.[42] Meanwhile during this period,

eleven countries were operating 22 launch sites.[43] More than 60 nations and

government consortia owned and operated satellites.[44] The U.S. share of worldwide

satellite exports dropped from nearly 2/3 in 1997 to 1/3 in 2008.[45] With the increase in

the number of providers and users of satellites, and the increased proliferation of launch

capable countries, there was also an increase in the development of ASAT and counter-

space capabilities.[46] The U.S. as the hegemonic presence in space was now at risk.

15

The preservation of the right to use space for the good of all mankind will be the space policy issue for the U.S. and the international community in the coming years. The space domain has become a significantly more challenging operating environment due to the lack of foresight in domestic and international space policy and law. There is an increasing effort by foreign parties to interfere with satellite operations. For example, in 2002, Iraq jammed U.S. positioning, navigation, and timing signals. In 2005, Libya and Iran interfered with international communications satellite transmissions that provided television to Arab nations. In 2006, China lased a U.S. imaging reconnaissance satellite. More recently, in January of 2007, China's successful test of a direct ascent ASAT weapon against a Fengyun 1C payload validated the threat to U.S. national interests in space.[47] Unless the international community changes how it manages space policy, the space domain could become unmanageable, dangerous, and unusable.

By mid-September 2010, the debris count from the Chinese ASAT test had reached 3,037 objects. Three and a half year later, ninety seven percent of the debris still remains in orbit after the test and is expected to threaten assets in space for the next 20 years. The debris from the ASAT test represents over 20 percent of all cataloged objects passing through low earth orbit.

Two years after this test, another disturbing event occurred. A "dead" satellite, Cosmos 2251, collided with an active communications satellite, Iridium 33. The debris field from the impact created over 1,750 objects. These two collisions increased the amount of space debris circling the planet by 60 percent (Figure 3).

To put these events in perspective, more than 4,700 space missions have been conducted since the beginning of the space age, and only 10 missions have accounted for one-third of all debris orbiting the earth. Alarmingly, six of these ten debris-producing events have occurred within the past 10 years.[48] The spike in the amount of debris from these two events mentioned above (Figure 3) created an entirely new dynamic in how the U.S. and the international community view this domain.

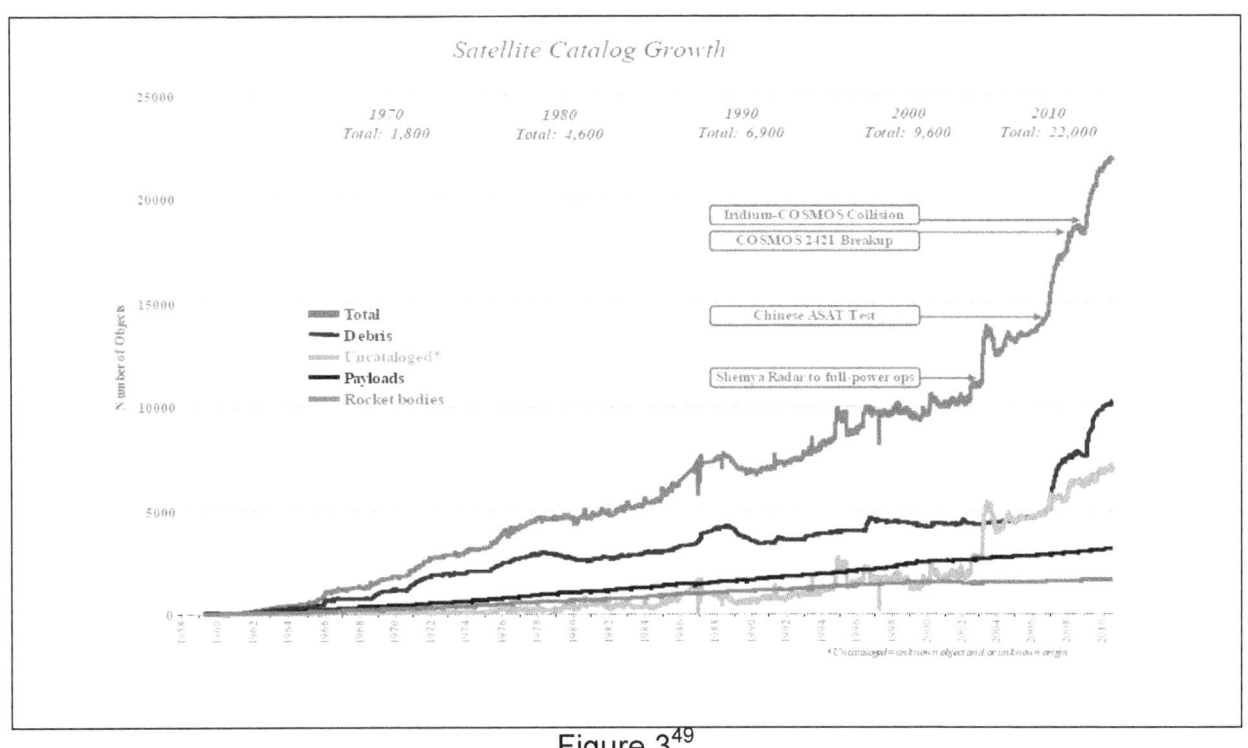

Figure 3[49]

Prior to the National Space Policy of 2006 the U.S. went a decade without a space policy. The policy in 2006 was a very passive policy essentially reiterating policy derived during the Kennedy and Johnson administrations. The policy deleted all references to U.S. efforts to develop missile defense and counter-space capabilities. Protection of U.S. assets was still included in the policy and stated the U.S. should "dissuade or deter others from either impeding those rights...take those actions necessary to protect its space capabilities; respond to interference; and deny, if necessary, adversaries the use of space capabilities hostile to U.S. national interests."[50] The Bush administration's unwillingness to address the emerging and current challenges occurring in the space domain could have significant impacts on national security.

President Obama's approach is very different from his predecessor. He has been aggressive with space policy by issuing the National Space Policy of the United States of America in 2010 and the National Security Space Strategy in 2011. In his space policy, President Obama addressed the contributions of civil and commercial space capabilities. "The United States is committed to encouraging and facilitating the growth of a U.S. commercial space sector that supports U.S. needs."[51] This is a reactionary policy to a problem that started to emerge in the late 1960s. As an example, the U.S. military leased 85% of the bandwidth from commercial satellite systems during Operation Enduring Freedom.[52] The military needed the bandwidth but military satellite communications can only provide a fraction of the requirement.

President Obama's current policy states that the U.S.'s "military and intelligence capabilities must be prepared to fight through a degraded environment and defeat attacks targeted at our space systems and supporting infrastructure."[53] Current policy now recognized the vulnerabilities to U.S. military satellites but without a proposed solution to the problem.

The U.S. advocated counter-space operations in the 1970s and 80s. Today the prestige of having a highly technical devastating weapon can catapult a country to the front and center on the world stage. China has demonstrated their ASAT capability and India is also developing an ASAT weapon.[54] The U.S. effort to develop an ASAT created a precedent for other countries. It is ironic that the concerns in the 2011 Space Strategy regarding operations in a degraded space environment were partly due to U.S. policies and 1970s and 1980s and U.S. ASAT capabilities. History has shown that other countries will emulate U.S. technology and space capabilities to further their national interests and increase their prestige, in some cases at the expense of U.S. national interests.

The lack of foresight concerning the space domain has left President Obama with no options than to accept commercial/civilian satellite support, and a potential adversary's counter-space capabilities as the current state of affairs. The U.S.'s inability to assess long term consequences of its policies has put U.S. national interests in space at risk. If civilian senior leadership had domestic processes that weighed past space policies and accounted for potential future effects of current policy, perhaps ASAT proliferation would not be a problem today.

Conclusion

In conclusion, presidents and their administrations lack of foresight established a reactionary short term view on space policy to the detriment of long term sustainability of space capabilities. When analyzing the origins of space policy, this lack of foresight is understandable. In the 1950s and 60s space exploration and the Cold War were intertwined. Rockets provided the U.S. with the ability to spy on the Soviet Union, enabled space exploration and led to the nuclear ballistic missile. Although President Eisenhower and President Kennedy were visionaries in their efforts to set the foundation to operate in space, their space policies were reactionary and they failed to understand the consequences of their policies. During the early years of space exploration, only the U.S. and Soviet Union exploited the space domain. The space domain had very few objects on orbit and the domain was only used for three purposes--exploration, spying and nuclear ballistic missiles. Policy was focused on winning the space race at the expense of a long view.

Although the utility and complexity of the space domain has slowly increased over the years, it seems subsequent U.S. administrations failed to adjust policy to keep pace with the change. Each administration's advocacy on space support and policy varied depending on the administration's personality and preoccupation. When an administration decided to develop a space policy, it seemed to start anew every time. Unfortunately, the pace of globalization and technology exceeded the U.S.'s ability to create effective space policy relevant to the changing conditions.

Even when administrations were focused on space, the lack of foresight in U.S. space policy could have an adverse effect on U.S. national interests in space. During President Reagan's administration, past U.S. led U.N. resolutions were ignored. The United States' development of the direct ascent ASAT weapon would provide a precedent leading to the Chinese testing their own ASAT weapon. This test created a debris field of over 3,000 objects. Even if a president's administration identified a negative trend, the trend was never addressed in policy. Most administrations' lack of foresight combined with little sense of continuity on space matters prevented U.S. leaders from seeing the long term effects of policy.

The international community needs an interagency process that provides expertise, and authority to recommend and enforce international space policy, treaties and laws. There are a number of international companies, consortiums and countries that have satellites in orbit, but there is no effective process to manage the space

20

domain. Many of the challenges that exist in space, for instance debris, are international problems which the UN does not have the authority to address. The U.N.'s five treaties and numerous resolutions focus primarily on the peaceful uses of space. There is no policy on the management of the domain with the exception of U.N. Resolution 2777, which addresses liability for damage caused by space objects.

There is no simple solution to the challenges of operating in space. As a start, there needs to be a process within the international community that provides dedicated expertise, authority and processes to manage all aspects of the space domain, similar to the International Civil Aviation Organization (ICAO). The U.N., in its current capacity, is not an adequate solution because it does not address the needs of consortiums and corporations that interact with the space domain.

The negative consequences of the status quo in space are clear. If the U.S. and the international community do not change how they manage this space domain, the future of space exploration is bleak.

Endnotes

[1] President Barack Obama, "Space Policy of the United States of America," June 28, 2010 http://history.nasa.gov/national_space_policy_6-28-10.pdf (accessed January 19, 2012), 1.

[2] Winston Churchill, http://www.brainyquote.com/quotes/keywords/history.html (accessed January 8, 2012).

[3] Deborah Cadbury, *Space Race, The Epic Battle Between America and the Soviet Union for Dominion of Space* (New York: Harper Collins, 2006), 4.

[4] Alexei Arbatov, and Vladimir Dvorkin, *Outer Space, Weapons, Diplomacy, and Security* (Washington D.C.: Carnegie Endowment for International Peace, 2010), 8.

[5] John L. McLucas, "U.S. Space Program Since 1961," in *The U.S. Air Force in Space, 1945 to the 21st Century* (Maryland: Air Force Historical Foundation, 1995), 82.

[6] Deborah Cadbury, *Space Race, The Epic Battle Between America and the Soviet Union for Dominion of Space* (New York: Harper Collins, 2006), 4.

[7] Ibid., 5.

[8] John C. Baker, Kevin M. O'Connell and Ray A. Williamson, *Commercial Observation Satellites at the Leading Edge of Global Transparency* (Arlington, VA: Rand, 2001), 20.

[9] C. Cargill Hall, "Civil-Military Relations in America's Early Space Program," in *The U.S. Air Force in Space, 1945 to the 21st Century* (Maryland: Air Force Historical Foundation, 1995), 21.

[10] McLucas, "U.S. Space Program Since 1961," 82.

[11] Alan Wasser, "LBJ's Space Race: What We Didn't Know Then (part 1)," *The Space Review*, Monday, June 20, 2005, http://www.thespacereview.com/article/396/1 (accessed December 12, 2011).

[12] The original text: He would rip out of the military those parts of it that were mainly devoted to fundamental rocketry or space research. Most notable of these were the Army's Jet Propulsion Laboratory at Caltech and von Braun's rocket team at the Redstone Arsenal in Huntsville, Alabama. Roger D. Launius, and Mike Gray, "Eisenhower," *Encyclopedia Astronautica, no date,* http://www.astronautix.com/astros/eishower.htm (accessed December 13, 2011).

[13] General Bernard A. Schriever, "Military Space Activities Recollection and observations," in *The U.S. Air Force in Space, 1945 to the 21st Century* (Maryland: Air Force Historical Foundation, 1995), 16.

[14] Erik Lander, Find a Grave, http://www.findagrave.com/cgibin/fg.cgi?page=gr&GRid=7553231 (accessed 13 March 2012)

[15] Wasser, "LBJ's Space Race."

[16] Clayton D. Laurie, "Congress and the National Reconnaissance Office" in *The Legacy History Series, June 2001* (Office of the Historian, National Reconnaissance Office, 2001) 2.

[17] Roger D. Launius, and Mike Gray, "Eisenhower," *Encyclopedia Astronautica, no date,* http://www.astronautix.com/astros/eishower.htm (accessed December 13, 2011).

[18] Sam Rayburn Speaker of the House of Representatives, Richard Nixon Vice President of the United States and President of the Senate National Aeronautics and Space Act of 1958 (Unammended) http://history.nasa.gov/spaceact.html (accessed December 14, 2011), Sec. 102. (a)

[19] Rayburn, *National Aeronautics and Space Act of 1958 (Unammended)*, Sec. 102. (b).

[20] John F. Kennedy, The President's Science Advisory Committee, *Report of the Ad Hoc Panel on Man-in-Space, December 16, 1960*, (NASA Historical Reference Collection, History Office, NASA Headquarters, Washington, D.C.), http://www.jfklibrary.org/Research/Ready-Reference/JFK-Speeches/Special-Message-to-the-Congress-on-Urgent-National-Needs-May-25-1961.aspx (accessed December 12, 2011).

[21] Compiled by the LBJ Library Archives Staff, "President Lyndon B. Johnson's Biography," Lyndon Baines Johnson Library and Museum National Archives and Records Administration, http://www.lbjlib.utexas.edu/johnson/archives.hom/biographys.hom/lbj_bio.asp (accessed December 12, 2011)

[22] The adhoc committee, consisting of the following countries: Argentina, Australia, Belgium, Brazil, Canada, Czechoslovakia, France, India, Iran, Italy, Japan, Mexico, Poland, Sweden, the Union of Soviet Socialist Republics, the United Arab Republic, the United Kingdom of Great Britain and Northern Ireland and the United States of America, was specifically asked to report on the following: (a) The activities and resources of the United Nations, of its specialized agencies and of other international bodies relating to the peaceful uses of outer space; (b) The area of international co-operation and programmes (sic) in the peaceful uses of outer space which could appropriately be undertaken under United Nations auspices to the benefit of States irrespective of the state of their economic or scientific development, taking into account the following proposals, *inter alia:*
> (i) Continuation on a permanent basis of the outer space research now being carried on within the framework of the International Geophysical Year;
> (ii) Organization of the mutual exchange and dissemination of information on outer space research;
> (iii) Co-ordination of national research programmes for the study of outer space, and the rendering of all possible assistance and help towards their realization;

(c) The future organizational arrangements to facilitate international co-operation in this field within the framework of the United Nations; (d) The nature of legal problems which may arise in the carrying out of programmes to explore outer space. *United Nations Resolution 1348, 13 December 1958*, http://unoosa.org/oosa/en/SpaceLaw/gares/html/gares131348.html (accessed Dec 13, 2011).

[23] McLucas, "U.S. Space Program Since 1961,"), 82.

[24] *United Nations Treaties and Principles on Outer Space* (U.N.ITED NATIONS New York, 2002), http://www.oosa.unvienna.org/pdf/publications/STSPACE11E.pdf (accessed December 10, 2011).

[25] *SP-4012 NASA Historical Data Book: Volume IV NASA Resources 1969-1978*, http://history.nasa.gov/SP-4012/vol4/ch1.htm (accessed December 12, 2011).

[26] Dr. T.S. Kelso, "Satellite Catalog (SATCAT)," http://celestrak.com/cgi-bin/search.pl (accessed December 12, 2011).

[27] President Jimmy Carter, "Presidential Directive –NSC 37, May 11 1978," http://www.marshall.org/pdf/materials/839.pdf (accessed December 14, 2011), 2.

[28] Ibid.

[29] This paragraph is a paraphrase of three separate sections of United Nations Space Law and Treaties. Incorporated is contextual timeliness of events and when these resolutions were passed. *United Nations Treaties and Principles on Space Law,* http://www.oosa.unvienna.org/oosa/en/SpaceLaw/treaties.html (accessed December 18, 2011)

[30] Ibid.

[31] Arbatov, *Outer Space, Weapons, Diplomacy, and Security,* 32

[32] Kelso, "Satellite Catalog (SATCAT)."

[33] "Historical Tables" from the Office of Management and Budget. (U.S. Government Printing Office, Washington D.C., 2004), http://www.gpoaccess.gov/usbudget/fy05/pdf/hist.pdf (accessed 12 December 2011). 76.

[34] NSDD-42, "National Space Policy, July 4, 1982," http://www.hq.nasa.gov/office/pao/History/nsdd-42.html (accessed December 12, 2011)

[35] Ibid.

[36] Lance Kawane, anecdotal evidence from personal experience from working the space surveillance mission at USSPACECOM/NORAD mission at Cheyenne Mountain Air Station, CO. 1996-1998.

[37] Ronald, Reagan, "Presidential Directive on National Space Policy," http://www.hq.nasa.gov/office/pao/History/policy88.html (accessed November 27, 2011).

[38] Ibid.

[39] President William Clinton, "Nation Space Policy 1996," http://history.nasa.gov/appf2.pdf (accessed December 14, 2011), 2.

[40] Daniel Gonzales, *The Changing Role of the U.S. Military in Space,* (Washington D.C.: Rand, 1999), 1.

[41] W. Henry Lambright, *Space Policy in the Twenty-First Century,* (John Hopkins University Press, 2003), 8.

[42] Kelso, "Satellite Catalog (SATCAT)."

[43] "Satellite," *Wikipedia,* http://en.wikipedia.org/wiki/Satellite#Launch-capable_countries (accesses December 12, 2011).

[44] Ibid.

[45] Ambassador Gregory L. Schulte, *A New National Security Strategy for Space,* "High Frontier, (February 2011, Volume 7, No 2) 6.

[46] Joint Futures Group (J59), *Joint Operating Environment 2010,* (Suffolk, VA: United States Joint Forces Command, February 18, 2010), 37.

[47] This is a paraphrase of numerous sections of Marc J. Berkowitz's article. Marc J. Berkowitz, *Protecting America's Freedom of Action in Space*," High Frontier (March 2011, Volume 3, No 2), 13.

[48] Brig Gen John W. Raymond and Mr. Kurt M. Neuman, *Preserving the Space Domain for Future Generations*, "High Frontier" (February 2011, Volume 7, No 2), 20.

[49] President Barack Obama, "National Security Space Strategy, January 2011," 1.

[50] President George W. Bush, "U.S. National Space Policy," August 31, 2006, http://history.nasa.gov/ostp_space_policy06.pdf (accessed December 15, 2011), 3.

[51] President Barack Obama, "Space Policy of the United States of America," June 28, 2010 http://history.nasa.gov/national_space_policy_6-28-10.pdf (accessed January 19, 2012), 3.

[52] Lance Kawane, 1999, 2000, 2006, Weapons School Graduate. Firsthand account from being a deployed Space Weapons Officer, integrating Space capabilities in Korea, Balkan CAOC, Air Component Command Element/Multi National Force-Iraq.

[53] President Barack Obama, "National Security Space Strategy, January 2011," 11.

[54] Peter D. de Selding, *India Developing Anti-Satellite Space Craft,* Space.com, January 11, 2010, http://www.space.com/7764-india-developing-anti-satellite-spacecraft.html (accessed January 19, 2012).